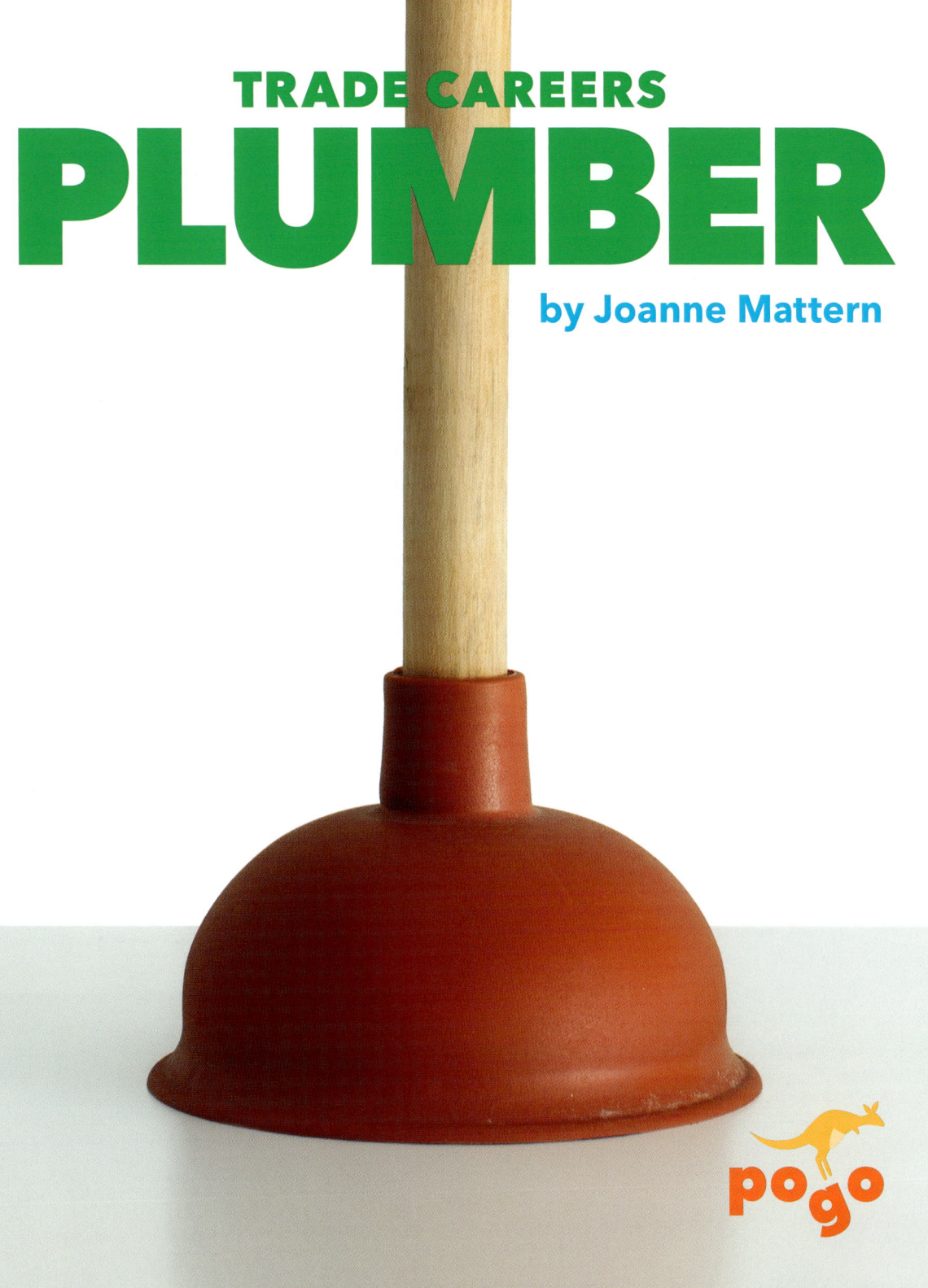

TRADE CAREERS
PLUMBER

by Joanne Mattern

pogo

Ideas for Parents and Teachers

Pogo Books let children practice reading informational text while introducing them to nonfiction features such as headings, labels, sidebars, maps, and diagrams, as well as a table of contents, glossary, and index.

Carefully leveled text with a strong photo match offers early fluent readers the support they need to succeed.

Before Reading

- "Walk" through the book and point out the various nonfiction features. Ask the student what purpose each feature serves.
- Look at the glossary together. Read and discuss the words.

Read the Book

- Have the child read the book independently.
- Invite him or her to list questions that arise from reading.

After Reading

- Discuss the child's questions. Talk about how he or she might find answers to those questions.
- Prompt the child to think more. Ask: Would you like to be a plumber? What do you like about this trade career?

Pogo Books are published by Jump!
5357 Penn Avenue South
Minneapolis, MN 55419
www.jumplibrary.com

Copyright © 2025 Jump!
International copyright reserved in all countries. No part of this book may be reproduced in any form without written permission from the publisher.

Library of Congress Cataloging-in-Publication Data

Names: Mattern, Joanne, 1963- author.
Title: Plumber / by Joanne Mattern.
Description: Minneapolis, MN: Jump!, Inc., [2025]
Series: Trade careers | Includes index.
Audience: Ages 7-10
Identifiers: LCCN 2024002640 (print)
LCCN 2024002641 (ebook)
ISBN 9798892131674 (hardcover)
ISBN 9798892131681 (paperback)
ISBN 9798892131698 (ebook)
Subjects: LCSH: Plumbing–Vocational guidance–Juvenile literature.
Classification: LCC TH6130 .M38 2025 (print)
LCC TH6130 (ebook)
DDC 696/.1023–dc23/eng/20240208
LC record available at https://lccn.loc.gov/2024002640
LC ebook record available at https://lccn.loc.gov/2024002641

Editor: Alyssa Sorenson
Designer: Anna Peterson
Content Consultants: Steven Gilmore, Plumbing Instructor, St. Cloud Technical & Community College; John D. Barber, Plumbing Technology Faculty, Hennepin Technical College

Photo Credits: ansonsaw/iStock, cover; Octavian Lazar/iStock, 1; adavino/iStock, 3; Woldee/iStock, 4; Andrey Popov/Dreamstime, 5; Pixel-Shot/Shutterstock, 6-7; Minerva Studio/Shutterstock, 8-9; BartCo/iStock, 10; monkeybusinessimages/iStock, 11; Image Source/iStock, 12-13; andresr/iStock, 14-15; grinny/Shutterstock, 16-17; Commercial RAF/Shutterstock, 17 (pipe wrench); vvoe/Shutterstock, 17 (plunger); DnDavis/Shutterstock, 17 (pliers); Victor Moussa/Shutterstock, 17 (drain snake); Freedom Life/Shutterstock, 17 (hacksaw); Mechanic3D/Shutterstock, 17 (blowtorch); Antrey/iStock, 18; CSA-Archive/iStock, 18 (logo); Hispanolistic/iStock, 19; sima/Shutterstock, 20-21; YinYang/iStock, 23.

Printed in the United States of America at Corporate Graphics in North Mankato, Minnesota.

TABLE OF CONTENTS

CHAPTER 1
What Is a Plumber?..4

CHAPTER 2
Learning the Trade......................................10

CHAPTER 3
Where They Work..18

ACTIVITIES & TOOLS
Try This!..22
Glossary..23
Index...24
To Learn More..24

CHAPTER 1

WHAT IS A PLUMBER?

Plumbers work with pipes. Pipes carry water and gas. They connect to homes, **factories**, and businesses. Plumbers put pipes in new buildings. They also fix pipes. When pipes are blocked, they **unclog** them.

TABLE OF CONTENTS

CHAPTER 1
What Is a Plumber? 4

CHAPTER 2
Learning the Trade 10

CHAPTER 3
Where They Work 18

ACTIVITIES & TOOLS
Try This! 22
Glossary 23
Index 24
To Learn More 24

CHAPTER 1

WHAT IS A PLUMBER?

Plumbers work with pipes. Pipes carry water and gas. They connect to homes, **factories**, and businesses. Plumbers put pipes in new buildings. They also fix pipes. When pipes are blocked, they **unclog** them.

Plumbers put in bathtubs, sinks, and toilets. They work with dishwashers and washing machines, too. These connect to pipes. That is how they get water.

CHAPTER 1　5

This toilet leaks. A plumber sees water dripping around the **bolts**. These attach the toilet tank to the bowl. She **drains** the tank. She sees the bolts are rusty. She replaces them. She fixes the toilet!

CHAPTER 1

TAKE A LOOK!

How does a toilet work? Take a look!

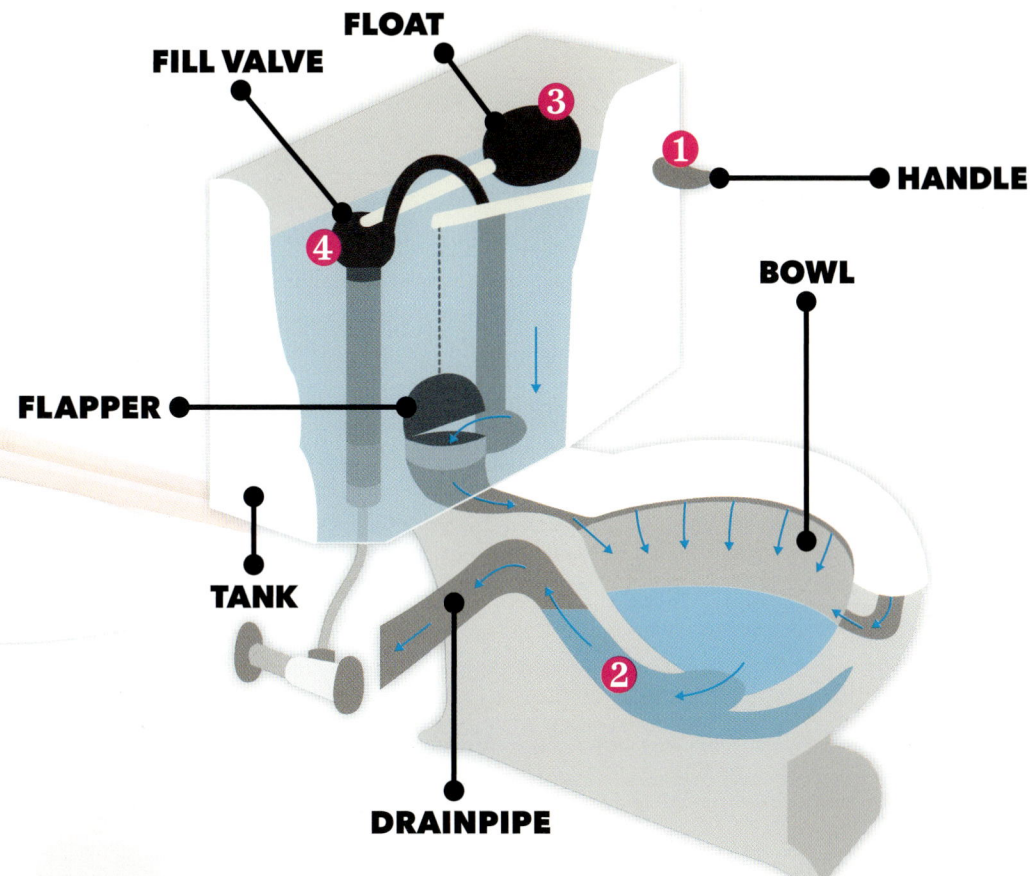

1. The handle presses down. The flapper lifts. Water in the tank goes into the bowl.
2. Dirty water in the bowl drains. It goes down the drainpipe. It goes to the **sewer**.
3. The float goes down when water leaves the tank.
4. The fill valve lifts. Water fills the tank. Some goes back into the bowl.

CHAPTER 1 | 7

A home needs a new **water heater**. It uses gas to heat the water. A plumber shuts off the gas. He turns off the water, too. Then he drains the tank. He takes off the attachments. These include the water and gas pipes.

The plumber takes out the old water heater. He brings in a new one. He connects everything to the water heater. He makes sure nothing leaks. The home has hot water again!

CHAPTER 1 9

CHAPTER 2
LEARNING THE TRADE

Do you want to be a plumber? First, you must graduate high school. Then you can take plumbing classes at a **vocational school**. You will learn about the **trade**. You will learn how to use tools, put in pipes, read **blueprints**, and more!

You can also be an **apprentice**. You will work with an experienced plumber. They will teach you more about the job. An apprenticeship lasts about four or five years.

apprentice

CHAPTER 2 11

After, there is a test. This proves how much you know about the trade. If you pass, you will get a **license**. This means you can work by yourself.

After more experience, you can take another test. Why? If you pass, you will be a master plumber. Master plumbers can run their own businesses. They make more money.

DID YOU KNOW?

Safety gear is important. Safety glasses protect eyes from chemicals or dirty water. Gloves keep chemicals away from hands. Face masks block mold or dust.

CHAPTER 2　13

Plumbers need good problem-solving skills. They have to figure out what is wrong. Then they find a way to fix the problem.

Communication skills are important, too. Plumbers tell customers what the problem is. They explain how they will fix it.

DID YOU KNOW?

Plumbing jobs can be physical. Plumbers often lift heavy objects. They may have to work in small spaces.

CHAPTER 2

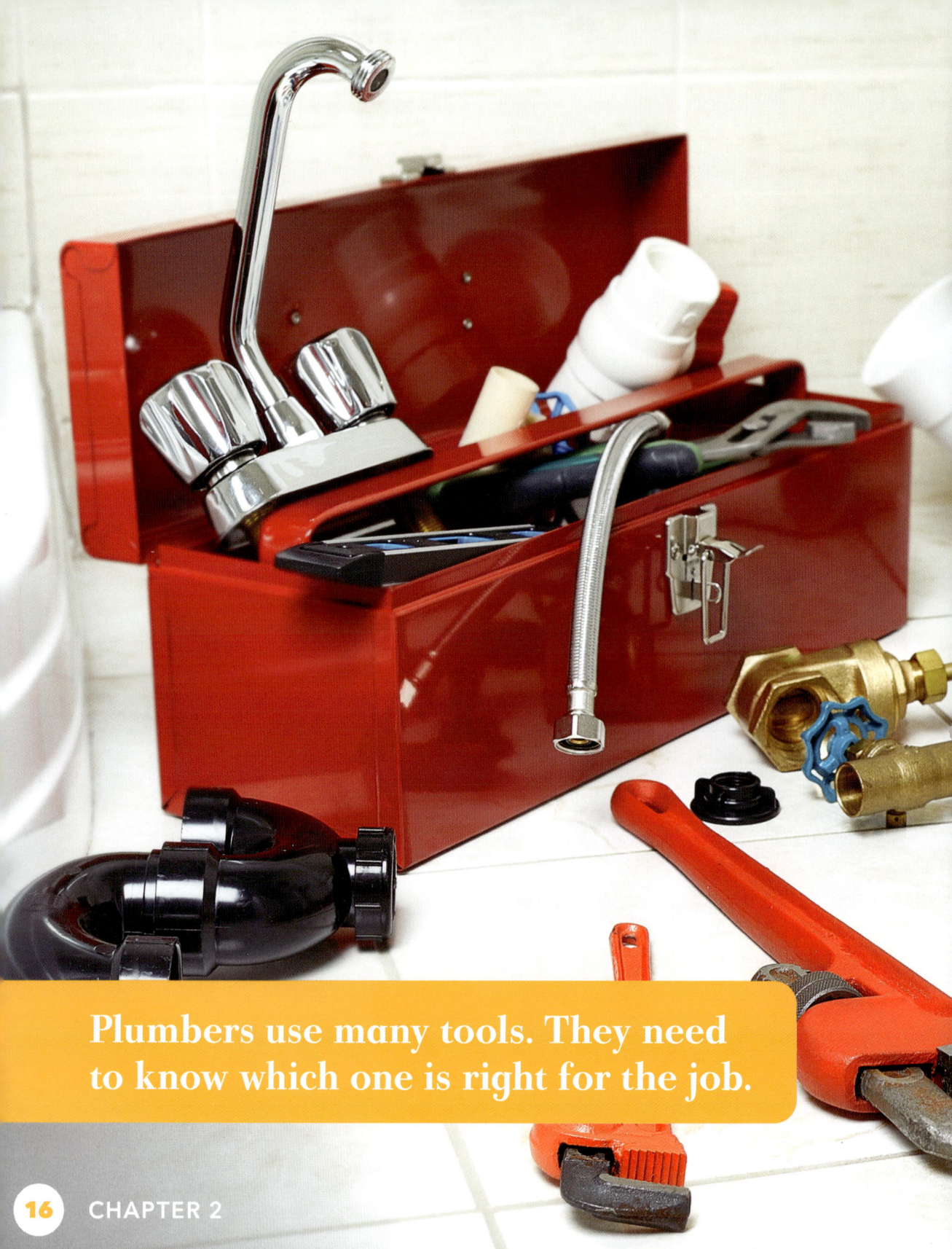

Plumbers use many tools. They need to know which one is right for the job.

16 CHAPTER 2

TAKE A LOOK!

What are some tools plumbers use? Take a look!

pipe wrench: tightens or loosens pipes and fittings

plunger: unclogs blocked drains and pipes

pliers: tightens or loosens small bolts and nuts

drain snake: removes objects that clog pipes

hacksaw: saws through metal pipes

blowtorch: melts material to join pipes together

CHAPTER 2 17

CHAPTER 3
WHERE THEY WORK

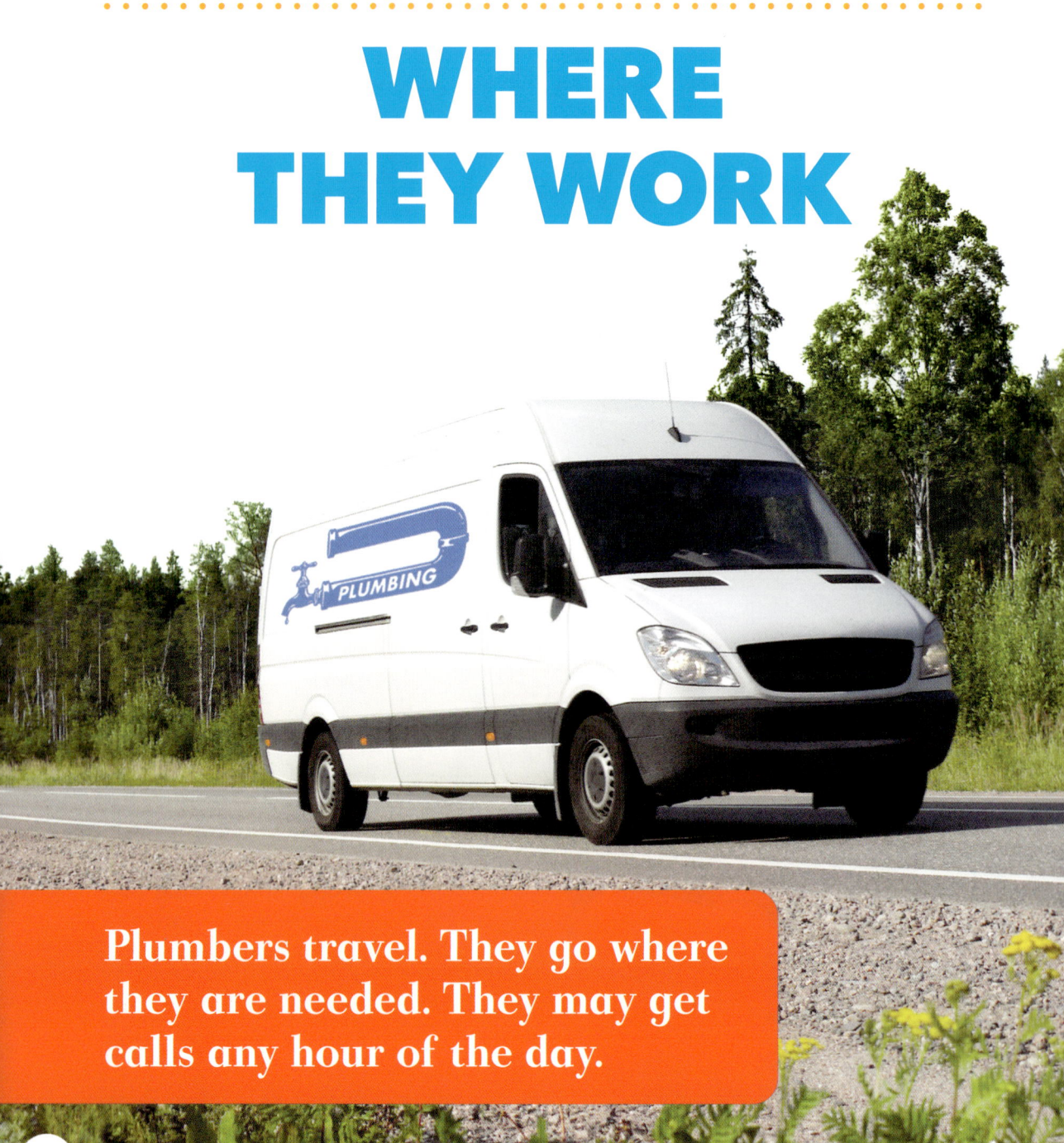

Plumbers travel. They go where they are needed. They may get calls any hour of the day.

Plumbers fix things in homes and businesses. Some work in large buildings like hospitals and malls. They put in pipes and drains. They make sure water systems work.

CHAPTER 3

Plumbers fix sewer lines. They also make sure gas lines are connected properly. Things like ovens and water heaters may need gas lines to work. Plumbers keep our world running!

DID YOU KNOW?

Plumbing can be dangerous. Hot pipes can burn. Sharp tools can cut. Plumbers have to be careful.

CHAPTER 3

ACTIVITIES & TOOLS

TRY THIS!

WHAT CAN YOU FLUSH?

Toilets get clogged. Why? People flush things water can't break down. These block pipes. What can and can't you flush? Find out with this fun activity!

What You Need:
- 4 glass jars with lids
- masking tape
- pen
- water
- wet wipe
- 1 Kleenex
- 2 sheets of toilet paper
- coin
- small toy
- Q-tip

1. Put a wet wipe in one jar. Put a Kleenex in another. Put two sheets of toilet paper in the third jar. Place the coin, small toy, and Q-tip in the last jar.
2. Label each jar. Use the masking tape and pen to write what is in each jar.
3. Put water in each jar. Fill them until they are almost full.
4. Screw the lids on the jars.
5. Shake each jar for one minute.
6. What items broke down in the water? What does this tell you about what you can and cannot flush down a toilet?

GLOSSARY

apprentice: Someone who learns a skill by working with an expert.

blueprints: Detailed design plans that show how something should be built.

bolts: Metal pins that screw into nuts to fasten things together.

drains: Removes liquid from something.

factories: Buildings in which products are made in large numbers, often using machines.

license: A document that gives someone permission to do certain work.

sewer: Underground pipes that carry away drainage water and liquid and solid waste.

trade: A job that requires working with the hands or with machines.

unclog: To remove objects blocking pipes and drains.

vocational school: A school that prepares students for trade careers.

water heater: A tank that stores and heats water.

INDEX

apprenticeship 11
attachments 8
blueprints 10
bolts 6, 17
communication 14
customers 14
dishwashers 5
gas 4, 8, 21
leaks 6, 8
license 13
master plumber 13

pipes 4, 5, 8, 10, 17, 19, 21
problem-solving 14
safety gear 13
sewer lines 21
sinks 5
toilets 5, 6, 7
tools 10, 16, 17, 21
travel 18
vocational school 10
water 4, 5, 6, 7, 8, 13, 19
water heater 8, 21

TO LEARN MORE

Finding more information is as easy as 1, 2, 3.

❶ Go to www.factsurfer.com
❷ Enter "plumber" into the search box.
❸ Choose your book to see a list of websites.

ACTIVITIES & TOOLS